The Book of Sleep

The Book of Sleep

Eleanor Stanford

Carnegie Mellon University Press
Pittsburgh 2008

Acknowledgments

Grateful acknowledgment is made to the following publications where these poems, or earlier versions of them, appear:

"Pisgah," *The Georgia Review*
"The Book of Sleep: A Picaresque," "The Book of Sleep (XIV)," *The Indiana Review*
"The Book of Sleep (X)," "The Book of Sleep (XVIII)," *Ploughshares*
"The Book of Sleep (IV)," "The Book of Sleep (XIII)," "The Book of Sleep (XV)," "'The World Was Created by Ten Utterances'," *TriQuarterly*
"February, Mid-afternoon: Nursing Ezra," *Poet Lore*
"Mudcloth (Côte d'Ivoire)," *Hotel Amerika*
"The Book of Sleep (III)," "The Book of Sleep (VIII)," "The Book of Sleep (XXXIV)," *Kalliope*
"The Book of Sleep (XX)," "The Book of Sleep (XXI)," "The Book of Sleep (XXV)," *Borderlands: Texas Poetry Review*
"The Book of Sleep (XXXIV)," *Literary Mama*
"The Book of Sleep (XIII)," "The Book of Sleep (XXX)," "The Book of Sleep (*West Mt. Airy*)," *Poetry International*
"Letter in July," *Margie*
"Throwing Barbie out the Window," "Self-Portrait, Cape Verde," "Political Poem," *Hunger Mountain*
"Málaga," *Rosebud*
"Darwin in the Cape Verde Islands," *Best New Poets 2005*

"Political Poem" was also featured on *Poetry Daily*.

Many, many thanks to my husband, Daniel Imaizumi; to my family; and to my teachers at the University of Virginia: Rita Dove, Charles Wright, Gregory Orr, and Lisa Russ Spaar.

Cover image: Haley Hasler, *Self-Portrait as a Mother*, 2004, oil on canvas, 48 x 36 inches

Book design: Rubén F. Quintero

The publication of this book is supported by a grant from the Pennsylvania Council on the Arts.

Library of Congress Control Number 2007931374
ISBN 978-0-88748-484-1

10 9 8 7 6 5 4 3 2 1

PENNSYLVANIA
COUNCIL
ON THE
ARTS

Contents

For Danny, Ezra, and Ruben

I

On the way to my wedding, I get lost

realize too late I've crossed the Ben Franklin Bridge
into Camden. The streets are empty. Dirty needles, broken glass,
the sun unwinding its bandages slowly. Longest hour
of the longest day of the year.

Cabral de Melo Neto wrote, *The river never opens up to fish.*
But he was speaking of a different river.

I always knew that I would marry a foreigner.
Or foring-er, as my mother-in-law says.

Cuica, birimbao: the band is playing a song
I almost recognize. What keeps breaking,
yet remains whole?

I always swore I'd marry a man who knew
what it is to miss something.

Those foringers. They are not afraid to wear their hearts
pinned to their powder blue tuxedos. They are not afraid
to appear ridiculous.

Self-Portrait, Cape Verde

It is better to say, 'I am suffering,' than to say, 'this landscape is ugly.'
                                    —Simone Weil

How dare you say the plow is beautiful?
Or the gnarled fist of manioc, the kerosene burned down
to a scorched wick?

The first person in Creole, you don't open your mouth.
N.   *N ta.*   *N ta bai*

How heavy this body has become.
The child who died of fever.
The velvet dress, earthen dance floor. Cigarette. I'm so tired
of translating.
                    Xan xinta li fuma nha cigarru—

It was never my knuckles against the washboard's ribs.
Or my grief, when the rain came,
and carried the pigs and goats into the sea.

The Book of Sleep: A Picaresque

Prologue, Foreword, Avertissement au Lecteur
Persons attempting to find a motive in this narrative, etc.
Chapter one. Cloud formations.
Chapter two. In which our hero nearly drowns attempting to swim
from São Felipe to Brava.
Chapter three. A short digression on Shark Fishing and
Classification.
Tiger, nurse, silvertip, gray reef.
Inflatable boat. Don't try it.
Atlantic sharpnose, spinner, milk.
We killed a goat on the beach, and its blood, dripping into
the ocean,
made the shark crawl up on the sand.
Chapter four. Dust storms. The road is lost.
Chapter five. Sossego. (Translator's note: This is harder
than it looks. How to convey the hush, the final vowel
that trails off? Insert here a pine tree, hillside blurred
in fog, those tiny yellow flowers . . . never mind.)
Chapter six. Fried manioc. Beans and hominy. Beer.
Chapter seven. You talk too much, like the little bird in the fig tree.
Chapter eight. Boiled-down papaya, coconut—even tamarind, if
you add
enough sugar. . . .
Chapter nine. My mouth, it doesn't work.
It can't give anymore.
Epilogue. Afterword. Retraction. In which we take it all
back. *Y los sueños, sueños son.*
"But to see you at my door again. . . ."

Ideogram

Above the forked branch, sound
flutters like a swallow. We live
in the moment's wicker cage, its hanging
house open to the wind. Snow slants
against the pane, the blank grid recalling
rice fields in Hokkaido. You trace
the curve of my cheek—first brushstroke
of a difficult character. In Japan,
where scholars spend a lifetime
learning how to write, it is the simplest words
that are the test of mastery: the bent twig
of a man, the four uneven beats of the heart.

February, Mid-afternoon: Nursing Ezra

The still water of his face:
the way expression
passes over it, his brow ruffled
by some distant storm. Next door
someone practices scales
on the trumpet, each note
a luminous balloon let go
above the neighborhood.
Where is the poem without ambition?
Even the trees preen
against the sky's flat mirror.
Even the glass of water on the table
trembles.

The Book of Sleep (III)

Early afternoon. I'm curled around you
like a snail. My words
circle; each swallows
its own tail.
The mobile, slowly
spinning, continues
to revise itself. It speaks
your language. Fish. Not
fish. Seahorse. Butter-
fly. *He built a little house, called*
a cocoon, around himself. He stayed inside
for two weeks.
                    Did he resist?
                              No.
                              He spun the silk strand
up his body and

Ezra at Six Weeks

Sleep, porous as cheesecloth,
lets light in. His cry a thin rope
that drags me up again and again.
Sun filters through the limbs
of the bur oak. Across the street
the Sudanese children wait
for the bus, poke the ground
with sticks, look injured.
What did they expect?
Not this. Certainly
not this.

Fontanel

Bruised peach,
pellucid
skullcap, trap-
door. I cannot be
gentle enough.

Backstroke

Ezra's curled up on my chest.
Observe the mother otter
with her young. . . .
Sleep's an infinite
recursion,
bodies burrowing
into the long afternoon.

All summer I practiced
diving off the board:
that moment before
you're airborne, toes
clinging to the rough,
testing its bounce.

The day undoes
a fine frizz
around my face
The body enters
its reflection:

We're a blur
of pleasure, pure
satiety.

Ezra at Ten Weeks

Beneath the window, umbrellas pass,
wheels of color on gray pavement.
In sleep, the knuckles find the mouth,
open, wet, comfort's imperfect
puzzle. I can't help it. All those years
I bathed on a hillside in the dark,
the tin cup of cold water,
ocean beating its palms on the black sand.

Málaga

The water flickers below the window.
Vines loose their fuchsia blossoms in my sleep,
and fog blooms across the pane.

All I remember is the words, how they moved like snakes,

shed their skin and glistened in the sun. The bay ripples,
spinning, an age-warped record.

A woman leans over the balcony, singing a bolero,
bright ribbons of sorrow trailing from her silk shawl.

The tide will swallow you until you learn
to let your body go, to swim back out on a pulse of blood.

Somewhere an accounting is being kept

So many pages dogeared: 115. 212.
As if the notched edge would hold
your place. As if you could go back.

But this morning, at that unspeakable hour,
the field wet, flowers like wineglasses
tipped over and forgotten in the grass,

the lawn chairs held their postures of attention
and surprise. At the foot of one, a rabbit: bearer
of bad news, furred messenger of the underworld.

The Book of Sleep (IV)

One half of the brain is always asleep.
The other treads its circadian rut.

      Thus it is written: Thou shalt lie down
in the clover field at noon. Thou shalt remove
thy watch and chain.

      In the pond, mallards bob
on sleep's surface and dip their heads, righted
by their heavy bodies.

      Thus the mothers who walk the gravel track
at dawn, always trying to lose
the last five pounds. Thus the empty
metal bleachers, the ducks conferring
on the wet grass by the long jump.

        Gonna lay down my sword and shield. . . .

The day is weightless until it descends with its webbed feet,
its countless loud demands.

Let Us Consider Carolus Linneaus.

Beginning with his name, so botanical
and florid, so perfectly
binomial. Let us consider
Linneaus in his study, quill poised,
white wig falling in curls
behind his ears. Or wearing
the brown-skirted costume
of Lapland, hand cupped
above the shaman's drum
at his waist. Or yet again
kneeling in the soil, digging in
the seeds for cacao, coffee, tea—
the planting itself
a species of prayer. Bananas,
rice, mulberries: all the crops
that failed him sooner or later,
when the fall came
with its flaming sword and beating wings
to usher him from the garden.

Nature's a butcher block, he said,
and perhaps it was
in Sweden, in the eighteenth century,
but in Charlottesville, Virginia,
in early June, it's more like a steam table,
heat rising from the ground,
everything garnished with green. Every morning
I strap my infant son to my chest
in the Baby Bjorn, a contraption native
to Linneaus' own Scandinavia, and we stroll
around the neighborhood,
our mouths thick with sounds,
examining the plants.

The Book of Sleep (VII)

The deer climbs into the yard at night.
I find her grazing in the garden. She lifts
her long neck and looks at me,
inquisitive.

tant' era pien di sonno a quel punto
che la verace via abbandonai

       I was so full of sleep. . . .

The Fifth Circle: New Jersey cul de sac,
sleepless women, hair unbrushed,
pushing strollers. Infants squall.
Cold spring drizzle. The wind
picks up.

These sidewalks lead nowhere.
And the cherry trees weeping on the wet grass,
and the swimming pools
still draped in their winter shrouds

A searchlight slashes its wide path. Hoof beat,
streak of blood on the hurricane fence.

And the Madonna with her long blue robe
And the Madonna with her sword of sorrow

Watching My Father-in-law Bathe Ezra

After dinner, dishes washed, sink sponged down
and gleaming, he tests the water on his wrist,
lowers you into the stainless steel basin.
He lathers the sun-brown arms and legs, pale curve
of belly, soft gathers of the genitals.
And the hands, dimpled stars
emanating light.

We all begin as immigrants.
But it is not without regret
that he cradles your small back.

The Asian pear on the table,
halved: its white-flecked skin,
delicate flesh.

He cups a palm to your forehead.
In answer you hold still,
and let the warm spray
rinse you clean.

"The World Was Created by Ten Utterances"

I realize suddenly that The Book of Sleep
has already been written
by someone else. I find it on the shelf, tattered, its spine
broken. I go to it gingerly, the way you came to me
after our son was born, as though you might tear me
open. Which you might have.

But the fireflies are blinking on, and I leave the book
facedown on the couch. There was the time
so many years ago when we filled a jar with them,
and let them go behind the shower curtain,
thinking the bathtub could be a lantern.

Or how when my brother was three he recited
his favorite joke over and over:
What's a bear without legs?
And answered himself, a frog.

Or the gardeners digging in azaleas, one singing
under his breath, *Así es la vida.*

It's not grunt work, my mother says, of the years
of naps and diapers and soggy graham crackers
behind the couch. *It's life.*

Or Nabokov: *Most of the dandelions had changed
from suns to moons.*

We don't have to think about that now.
About how in a few months,
we'll stand in synagogue,
hit our chests with our fists, and ask Adonai
to write us into The Book of Sleep for another year.

II

Letter in July

We spent the afternoon sitting on a blanket on the floor,
fitting plastic cups inside each other, building a tower,
knocking it down. I heard Berryman's mother admonishing,
'To confess you're bored means you have no Inner Resources.'
And my own mother, when I was bored:
"Go bang your head against the wall."

Summer is another thing. Humid and dumbstruck, we return
to childhood. We walk the dog. We feed the chickens. In the
                                                    evening,
a thunderstorm beats the zucchini in the garden to the ground.
I am afraid of the suburbs, of their unearthly quiet,
rain-drenched hydrangeas blushing in the yard,
rusty nails buried at their roots.

In a Palestinian poem, I find the line, *Farewell,
small island of ours.*

Today I fed the baby his first taste
of solid food. I mixed rice cereal with breast milk
and lifted it on my finger to his mouth. The flakes a lunar confetti
scattered in the bowl. He made a face and swallowed:
half celebration, half a spoonful of regret.
Farewell, small island of ours.

When Berryman jumped from a bridge in Minnesota,
his name billowed out behind him like a cape. But did not stop
his fall. If he did not think of his mother in Oklahoma,
I think of her now, rolling out biscuit dough, stamping it
into circles with a glass, confessing nothing.

The Book of Sleep (VIII)

I see it in my son's face, that fear, the moment
when the swing is suspended, when gravity
releases him. Who holds him
then?
      Not I.

      Not I said the hen. And dusk
like a scattering of grain on the henhouse floor.

Let us read now from the Book of Sleep:
     And at the evening sacrifice I arose up
from my heaviness—

The clocks spin forward. Five, six, seven.
Fear is crepuscular. But tell that
to the chickens huddled under the sky's
gray roof.

     Don't leave me alone in the twilight. . . .

When fear wakes him like that, arms thrown out
as though to embrace it, I want to apologize,
I want to get down on my knees
and beg forgiveness.

Pisgah

We woke in the field
and found the fence down, nothing between us
and the cows. They were thinking deeply
about the grass. Their stomachs
four-chambered, like hearts.

Driving west into Tennessee, the fog
glittered like mica. The wedding glasses,
packed in paper, rattled in the trunk.
The words were all so inexact.

But years later, you said, remember the fog,
how it was like pressing the palm of your hand
to your closed eyelids until stars appeared,

and I said yes, I remembered it.

The Book of Sleep (X)

The field believes profusely in its weeds.
Who are we to intervene?

Each evening lasts for days.
We play whist and euchre on the porch.
We practice sleeping without closing our eyes.

Season of bing cherries and stained teeth,
of unfenced cows lowing along the highway.

And the river like a long dream,
erasing its banks.

I'm goin' down in it three times
pebble rolling over in the blue-
green shallows
But Lord   I'm only comin' up twice

Nashville

We stand outside the full-scale replica
of the Parthenon. The only in the world, the sign
assures us.

The brilliant ruins, white pillars of sun
toppled in the grass.

Under the glossy leaves of the magnolia,
the baby falls asleep in my arms. What souvenir—
key chain, guitar pick, plastic Dolly figurine—
will remind us who we were before?

The cradle rocks above an abyss.
But this space
whistling inside my chest—

All over the city, the musicians
are just waking up. Clearing their throats,
testing their heart-wrenched yodels.

Deciduous

Cusp of next season pushes through
the rim of Blue Ridge. Late August,
Ezra cutting a new tooth, and night's
one long wail, its dark mouth
open, the dull comfort
of whiskey on the gums.

        It's a slow
wearing down, sweat gathering
at the temples.

Then fall:
        pulp and root, this crown
of thorns
             lord lord

And the cicadas beating their wings,
clinging to the trees. . . .

Political Poem

While the President is speaking about security,
I am straining peas through the food mill, splattering
the kitchen counter with green specks. The radio is on
at a low volume, so I will be less tempted
to throw things at it, but instead I just grind harder,
until my fingers are pressed against
the metal holes, threatening to grate the skin
from my knuckles. If this were another country, somewhere
in Latin America, say, or Eastern Europe, I could write lines like,
My country, take care of your light!, as Neruda did,
I could write, *I am begging you the way a child*
begs its mother, as he did, staring out his window
at the ocean tiresomely reiterating on the black rocks.
Oh, to live among those writers
who make unabashed use of vodka
and exclamation marks! Except in such a place
I would probably be the one lost in the steam
of a pot of boiling cabbage, I would be the one
with a baby tied to her back and her hands
busy on the tortilla board, flattening anger
into perfect floured circles. As here in my kitchen full
of modern appliances, I push my anger through
the metal strainer, and prepare to feed it by small spoonfuls,
mixed with rice cereal and breast milk, to the baby.

The Book of Sleep (XIII)

Gustinha's memorized The Book of Sleep, recites
long passages in her head while she beats the clothes
against the washboard.

And so Gurete in the kitchen, Nunena in the fields,
Nha Nha hauling water in a bucket on her head.

The roster echoes off the schoolhouse walls:

Jeiza, Fátima, Lila, Teté.

Not here, not here, not here, not here.

A thin film of kerosene keeps the mosquitoes
from breeding in the well. Soon you learn
to swallow it, to crave its dark iridescence
on your tongue.

The Book of Sleep (XIV)

At least this is a country someone's
heard of. At least the soldiers at the airport are polite
as they rifle through the luggage. They keep only the bag of
$$M\&M's.$$

I saw the factory where they make these trinkets—
$$machines$$
weaving the baskets, refugees stitching kente cloth shirts,
whirring, glue stench, cheap wooden masks
with their identical blank stares:
There's a pattern here. Heat and dirt,
dysentery and paranoia, rain every afternoon at four.

*Two hundred francs? One-fifty? I'll throw in my pocketknife
for those sandals—*

The postcards on the wire racks, faded, already scribbled with
$$messages$$
before I buy them, dust-smeared, grease from other people's
$$fingers.$$

At least they have postcards here.

I address one, write, *I'm trying to learn the game with the rows
of little stones. I can't keep up with the old men in the bar.
My pile of pebbles keeps diminishing.*

At night, my dreams stand up and walk around the room.
The bed sheets in the hotel have been washed so many times
they can't be clean.

This watch? It stopped working months ago. Time's
a jeweled insect creeping up my wrist.

The boulevards are choked with traffic and exhaust. The taxi
                                                                    drivers
always overcharge. The book in my back pocket wrinkled and
                                                                    heat-swelled.
      Page 42: *Everywhere the exile kneads the bread of tears.*
Lamb shank, monkey fruit, zouk pulsing from the storefronts.
Faith hangs its flag at every door: green cedar, sickle and star.
Men lie down in the street at noon to pray.

The Book of Sleep (XV)

All night I waited at the edge of the gallery-forest.
I dreamed the lion with your bloody cloak in his mouth.
I dreamed the river swallowed you, your body
a small bulge in its throat.

This place where I live now, it is a country
whose name has changed many times.
A country whose present status
is not clear.

By the sleek surface of the lake,
the cattle flick their tails,
bend their large heads to drink.

On the road I saw a beautiful girl,
carrying a clay urn on her head.
She balanced it so casually,
I knew it was full, and knew
that whatever it contained
was all she had.

New Jersey Transit

We creak north out of Philadelphia: Bridesburg, Elizabeth,
Rahway. The book falls open on my lap.
Every place I've lived rumbles beneath the floor.

Lorca says to Whitman, *Sleep; nothing remains.*

You know what you'll be staring at
when you wake up: row houses, basketball hoops, above-ground
swimming pools. The children floating glassy-eyed
and silent. The sign on the bridge should read
Trenton makes the world takes, but it's missing the final *t*.
The world aches.

Where we're headed, carp trace slow circles
in the windows. Immigrants hawk cheap watches on the street.
When it rains, the umbrellas bloom, sudden sea anemones.

But first, the dark tunnel, jostle and stutter,
conductor calling last and final stop. Behind me,
a woman's voice repeats, *Gracias a Diós. Gracias a Diós.*

The Book of Sleep (XVIII)

You drove all night through thunderstorms, the PA turnpike
slick and narrow in the passes. The tractor trailers roaring,
and sleep
whistling past your ears. . . .

My heart was where a hundred roads
  converged & then moved on

        At one point you drove under a mountain.
Later the sun unfolded over the hills,
and you realized the rain had stopped.

You found me on the shore of Lake Erie.
At my feet a million prehistoric animals offered up
their calcified bodies.

Presque Isle, it was called.

We held hands in the dark theater. A woman read a book
in a sparsely furnished bedroom. Ants crawled across
an open palm.

        Then you left, and again the dull sun, the clock
parceling out the hours. Again the nuns tending the gardens
in their sad habits.

The Refugees

They sleep in the basement, and play memory
late at night: cards slapping the table
in complicated rhythms. Arabic wail from the radio.

They always keep score.

One is an Olympic table tennis champion.
One is a dwarf.
One tended goats in his village.

Their language is one I understand
but cannot speak. It is the language
of my father, of the place he left before I was born.

I am mute and useless as the flat jute faces
on the wall. Even the parakeets
can speak it.

But the words in my mouth are afraid
to leave, afraid they will not find their way
back. So I swallow them:

dorowat; amhari; injera
spread with clarified butter; the lamb stew
we eat with our hands.

The Book of Sleep (XX)

All night it is raining or about to rain. I listen
to my parents' records on the old turntable: "Abbey Road,"
"Blood on the Tracks," "The Last Waltz." Outside, the hydrangea
breathes quietly in the grass.
Kabir says, If you have not lived through something,
it is not true.

        Careful, my parents say. That's your inheritance.

The Book of Sleep (XXI)

At my bat mitzvah, I read from The Book of Sleep.
I stand on the bimah, shaking in my lace shawl.
Any day now, any day now,
I shall be
released
The congregation nods off, one by one.

       Then the chorus girls and disco lights. Then the magician
pulling my future out of his hat, the salmon spread and challah,
the gangly thirteen-year old boys drunk on kosher wine.
Then the balloons with my name on them
floating toward the ceiling. . . .

Throwing Barbie out the Window

Remember when you cut off your Barbie's hair
and threw her out the window? The sequined bodice
flashing in the sun, the sharp heels of her go-go boots
The vertiginous heights,

                                    the plummeting

Remember when you dropped acid
by the swimming pool
and your hands became the leaf-shadows
on God's clear blue mind

Then the airplane coming down gently,
how you threw your fear into the wind, and it opened
like a parachute

Remember the wind singing against the cliff?
Gustinha filling the cornmeal *pasteis* with fish,
saying something about *vida di pobri*—
this poor life—and how finally the words
were not words, but something else

The Book of Sleep (XXIII)

We wake into a body, into the cold shock
of the swimming pool. Sleep
guards the perimeter: flip-flops lined up
on the deck, day lilies still covering their eyes
with green hands.

Skin peels from shoulder blades.
On the empty lawn chairs, cicadas
shed translucent wings.

The mole above the right knee, its dark
lunar face. And Rachel, whose left arm ends
just past the elbow—

Try not to stare.

The black lines on the bottom waver. The arm
traces a keyhole beneath the chest. Fingers drag
and catch, palm cupped.

Water pleats, its flutter like crinoline.
*The duende rises up from the soles
of the feet*, but sleep

The Book of Sleep (XXV)

On each corner, the braceros wait for the day's labor
to swoop down on them—flatbed, pitch and tar,
shovel's iron head.

In the Upanishad of Sleep, Sauryayani Gargya asks,
Who enjoys the mystery of sleep with no dreams?

Only the opossum, ugly and scuttling in the dark.
Only the accordion, which folds back into its own cry,
            and thus has no need of dreams.

But in the city of the body, the fires are burning.

In the taqueria on North Congress, the waitress
wipes down the tables with a rag. The sky
already white and unforgiving,
the smell of scorched flour on her hands.

Darwin in the Cape Verde Islands

I.
In the market, a woman grabs my arm
to sell me unfamiliar fruits. I hold an apple
in my palm no bigger than a peach stone.
My money has no value here. Take
my cufflinks: they are useless
as a pair of dung beetles, silver exoskeletons
glinting in my outstretched hand.

A man can't trust his senses.
The clarity that draws the hills in sharp relief
is nothing like the clarity
of home. Young girls in bright shawls
flutter like a circle of doves, winged palms
beating time on their thighs. What instrument
can measure this aerial transparency? Not
the hygrometer; not the swift pulse
of blood, the needle of my compass, quivering.

II.
It's a delirium, this haze that descends
westward from the continent. How
to judge this happiness that descends
in a fine silt upon one's shoulders? How
to echo the sparse beauty, the lava fields
a single sprig of green would spoil?
If indeed, a person who's seen fields
of lavender on the horizon, the spoils
of too long away from land, can judge.
In the market, a slab of tuna fresh from sea
rests on a woman's head. Its flesh is judge
of what the day will yield: a placid sea,
pink-bellied sky. Who that has just walked
for the first time in a grove of cocoa-nuts
will question that a fish as well has walked

on two legs from the sea? The cocoa-nuts
rattle in the wind, and shake the dust
from their sharp fronds; his own happiness
flutters like a compass. How to shake the dust
from this strange body, to own this happiness?

III.
Dear Reader, for what novel aspects have we scoured
the globe, only to long for our own gardens, sour
cherries and seckle pears, the orderly rows
of thyme and marigolds? Still, everything grows
from something else, and these plots we mind tend
toward propagation. The missives that I send
will find my wife knitting by the fireside.
Does she undo her stitches every night,
while I lose my own steps in this dust?
At the old church, colored flags flutter
and an ancient priest mumbles blessings
in strange Portuguese. Outside, the wind threshing
the banana leaves repeats itself. But, Reader, dear,
the final page remains unwritten here:
This earth offers no certainty for cows or goats
or the acacias in their dusty coats, growth
stunted by the trade winds. The fine dust broke
our instruments; it gathers on the masthead, chokes
the sun. It comes from Africa; and why
should this surprise? We have traveled farther, blind
to what has brought us here. Leave India, its teas
and silks and spices, to others. The tree
of knowledge grows in more barren climes;
all I seek is this: a way to unwind time,
to trace the story to its roots. The women,
black as jet, watch us with their inky
eyes. What secrets do they weave into the bright
cloths they tie about their hips? They hide

intention in a blur of dance. The youngest girls
know how to move like that, how to twirl
their bodies to the frantic song. These islands
breed an instinct for survival: the silent
lizards with their darting tongues and bulging
eyes; the cuttlefish, chameleon-like, divulging
nothing but a blur of ink in its wake.
It's a rare species of happiness that takes
here. Reader, it confounds my science;
if it has a name, perhaps it's *transience*.

Fogo

In the stone quintal, Nireida hacks off her Barbie's hair
with a machete. The air's a honed blade.
Steep fields of manioc and sweet potatoes,
and halfway down the mountain, the outline
of the boy they call Nomi, which means
Name.

It is lovely to be so literal, to feel the nubs of words, the dirt
clinging to their roots.

At the bar, under the thatched roof of sky,
the blind man is playing the violin. The song that goes,
My knife is sharpened,
My pan is washed.
The goat's tied up
behind the shed.

Clarity of Santo Antão;
memory of sun etched into our backs.
We asked for an evening
clear as this.
We'll eat the goat
with fried manioc and greens.

The Book of Sleep (XXVI)

The nineteenth century was exhausting.
The texts of moral philosophy, their pages
crisp as the pink crepe myrtles in the garden.
                    So much self-improvement,
the little books in which we tracked our progress.

Even now, a heaviness
besets me.
                    Let us rest a moment in the shade
of the umbrella magnolia.

And observe the Reverend McGuffey,
reading aloud from his McGuffey Reader—
Bess in her goat-pulled cart—to the children
sprawled beneath the generous limbs
of the silverbell.

The pocket watch tucked away
inside its fob, its face hidden.

The Book of Sleep (XXVIII)

Open it to any page:
you've been here before, these quiet streets, each house
waving its own flag, the men in shirtsleeves
watering the lawn. Hollyhocks lean against the fences,
hands to their foreheads,
souffrante.

So this is the chapter in which childhood
is recounted: not yours necessarily.
The boys on the blacktop of St. Margaret's,
throwing the ball again and again
at the hoop. The girl jumping rope who stopped you
on the street, her face radiant, and asked
if she could pet your dog, she loves dogs.

This is the chapter in which we lay our hands on the table.

That card game we used to play
where the loser gets his knuckles rapped—
no one remembers the rules, only
the stiff edges of the deck
flaying the skin.

Teaching Sixth Grade at Incarnation

The small heads bent over their textbooks
as though in prayer: Stephanie James, Jack Durocher,
Claire Connolly with her soccer jersey
and blond hair.

Saint Gertrude, patron saint of exiles and Jews,
    pray for us now and in the hour—

It's an uneasy truce, the cross
nailed above the blackboard. Outside,
the Blue Ridge illuminated by the October afternoon,
trees gilded. Leaves of a prayer book fluttering open.

Years of Hebrew school have taught me: it's not the words
that matter.

Hour of Algebra. Homeroom. History.
11:44, Hour of Lunch and Recess. Glory Be.

For biology, we parse the margins of the school,
the subdivision trellised with gentian and orange hawkweed
We prepare slides for the microscope, tiny scrolls
of birch bark and leaf mold.

We all know the Pope's position:
evolution is permissible. Just don't
mention the soul.

Strange animals: mantis and tarantula,
dragon lizard in the glass terrarium—
we watch in awe. From whence
are you descended?

Crashing the Ringling Gala, Sarasota

We swam up from the dark.
Stench of red tide and strands of seaweed
clinging to our limbs like phosphorescent dresses.
Invisible in the glow of tea lights on the lawn,
we glided among the swish of ball gowns
and the clinking of crystal.

Greek statues stretched out their white arms to the gulf.
The grass ran right up to the water and lay down at its feet.

A lizard lifted its head, opened a delicate green fan.

We were weightless then.
We somersaulted over everyone's head,
arcing the sky's black tent.
Outside, the shouts from the dog track
spun in wider and wider circles.
Just beyond, the airport's blue lights
blinked, guiding us gently down.

The Book of Sleep (XXIX)

The chameleon
unzips
his slick suit,
slips each
short leg
into the new one.

III

Mudcloth (Côte d'Ivoire)

The man is wearing his animal head.
He carries a torch in one hand,
a whip in the other.
The waterfowl on one reedy leg
tilts back her head. The fish
ascends sky's ladder.
Our hands hang at our sides
like bells. Our feet sound their song
on the hard earth.

Marriage

In the picture, the man is cutting down the old tree.
He balances at the edge of one
abbreviated branch, end of the limb caught
in mid-air,
falling.

I imagined he would fell it
with one cut, take a chainsaw
to the trunk.

Instead we had to watch it come down
one piece at a time.

You stood there in your yellow garden clogs
and cried.
I was the one with the camera.

It was early, the street empty of cars,
fog lifting, and for a moment
it seemed we were someplace else,
somewhere less suburban,
wilder.

The Book of Sleep (XXX)

Truth or Consequences, NM)

The woman with the long gray braid
and the silver charm at her ankle
lowers herself
into the concrete tub.

The scar on her right arm—small scythe,
half-smile. Of all the men who have traced
its Braille in her skin, not one could read in it
the arc of tree branches knocking on the window
of her girlhood, or the long line
of children in the gym
waiting for their inoculations

Above the tub, a rope of ancho chilis
sways like silent
shriveled chimes. These springs
originate someplace else, and if they emerge here
and soften her skin with sweat and sorrow,
it is not intentional.

The Sleep of Cotyledons

1.
She decided she would live simply,
doing without sleep. Then the objects
in the boudoir began to taunt her: beveled
mirror, jewelry box, vanity.

2.
And the graceful nyctitropic movements
of her palm—upward
and downward, fronds
incurved

3.
perhaps the central bud or plumule

4.
I fell into a deeply paradoxical sleep.

5.
Fig. 125, *Diurnal and nocturnal positions
of the cotyledons*

6.
Bundled with my betrothed, we tossed restlessly,
hats and gloves, the tassels of our scarves
tangling.

7.
Thus the peasants of South Europe
fear for their olives. Thus the thin covering
of straw, the fruit trees along the garden wall.

8.
Fig. 125A, *The first true leaf.*

9.
But if we hold our hands motionless
before a fire

Changing Ezra, 2 a.m.

The map above the changing table
holds him in its thrall. His scream
hovers, then dissolves, a squall
dissipating over the South Pacific.
All he sees is contrast: one country
blurs into the next.

The plates are shifting.
They drift toward each other,
away from that mutable ocean
where once he swam so fluently.

Remember the garbage barge that left New York
and sailed halfway around the world,
only to return to harbor?
Even Haiti couldn't be convinced to take it.

Geography is finite, that's the problem.

But night—its borders are permeable, his cry
the coyote that ferries me across.

The Insomnia Studies

for J.

They hook you up to the electrodes,
slip on the helmet, lower you
into the mines. You're given: a pickax,
small cone of light, enough rope
to hang yourself. A small blue pill
to allay the fear.

What helps? Needlepoint: knit one, purl two,
clickity click. Also, statistics. Chapter four:
Spurious Correlations.

You moved here so you wouldn't have to drive,
and now look: the subway rattles
like a caged animal. People live down there, you know.
They say the eyes adjust. They say
you can even read. Page 81: *Being invisible & without
                substance, a disembodied voice*

The ancient Greeks believed sparrows dug themselves
into the ground for the cold months. What did they think
the birds were doing? Sleeping? Or playing cards
and eating spanakopita, waiting for spring?

The Book of Sleep

(West Mt. Airy)

In the kitchen, you lay down your crowbar,
breathe in the dust
of someone's asbestos-choked childhood.
Clouds wander in the hole
where the window used to be.

On Germantown Ave., the goatherd
leads his flock past the pizza place
and video store. Hurried neither
by the honking cars, nor by the threat of snow.

In time, all creatures
should be hid under the cloud of forgetting

And thus sleep, so long
deferred, guts us, takes down
the parting walls.

Boca

Air conditioning clatters
against the slatted blinds; below,
the intercoastal, ribbed with docks,
the lizards darting their quick tongues.

The whorled interiors,
the moon snail, bleeding tooth,
erato.

We're not opposed to consequences.
Nothing here has calories.
We idle our motors
endlessly, forgetting
our errands.

Nights are a flat expanse of ocean,
a mirage. The first three stars
that mean day's begun.

And the ten thousand stars invisible:
ambient reflection, failing eyes,
yahrzeit.

Machu Picchu

And the grinding bad luck of everyday was
like a black cup that they drank, with their hands shaking.
                                        —Neruda

Once we wrote each other letters from different
islands: you on São Vicente, watching the boats
come in and leave, me on Fogo, waiting for the volcano

to erupt. Now you send me a postcard from Machu Picchu—
mossy peaks, and inside, the ancient city, hidden
from the Spanish for a thousand years. Peru

is the new Cape Verde, you write, and perhaps
it's true. How long can I keep strolling around this same praca
in my mind, the chipped statue of Amilcar Cabral,

poet and liberator? Even he fought the war of independence
somewhere else. And the old women, dressed in black,
waiting for their ships to come in—

Someone should tell them too. Quit squinting at the horizon.
                                        Cast off
those dark-hued headscarves. Put down the black cup
trembling in your hands.

The Book of Sleep

(Somnus Plantarum)

In the garden of lost vegetables, it is always
August. Under the branches of the chaste tree,
we make our rectilinear bed. And lie in it.

Sleep is a rose, the Persians say. But in Virginia
we say it is an heirloom plum, its flesh
the dark blush of a cheek, turning away—

In the garden of lost vegetables, it is always
the nineteenth century. Age of the forward pea
and serpentine cucumber.

We have other ways of telling time:
Along the wall, the pomegranate and fig
with their complicated seeds.
And the sleep-at-noon, and the punctual
four-o'clocks, nodding off by five. . . .

The Book of Sleep (XXXIV)

There is no such thing as a baby.
—D. W. Winnicott

It was winter. All around, the mountains
like an open mouth, preparing to speak.

I said your name over and over, as though
this could help. Ah, little fish, slick-bodied
fingerling. Names have nothing to do with you.

A cloud passes over the moon.
Strokes its pocked cheek gently, then
moves on.

The baby monitor picks up strangers'
telephone conversations. *Nothing
you can do about it now,*
the woman says.

There's no book where it's written down.
All those hours, blank pages blowing
across the snowy steppes. Your body leaves
its imprint in the wrinkled sheets:

shape that won't fit you anymore
come evening.